THIS

IS

MY

HOME

Facts compiled by Nancy Zimmerman

Illustrations by   Ian Dayton

HEDGEHOG HILL PRESS

An imprint of NJZ Enterprises

NJZ Enterprises
PO Box 3148
Anderson, IN 46018

www.nzbestself.com

A Hedgehog Hill Press Original, 2018

ISBN: 978-0692066898

DEDICATION

It is my pleasure to dedicate this book to the talent of Ian Dayton. It has been great working with him and I hope that you enjoy the talent of this fourteen year old young man as much as I do.
                                                Nancy Zimmerman

I want to dedicate this to the waitress at Steak N Shake that referred me to Nancy, Abbie Holmes.
                                                Ian Dayton

(Ian Dayton has avidly drawn characters and played piano from a young age. A homeschooled Washington, Indiana native, he was born in 2003. He is the youngest of six which has resulted in creating quite a comedian in the family and this just happens to be his first book. If you wish to get in touch with Ian, he can be reached through the publisher of this book.)

Preface

You will notice that there is space at the end of some of the pages of facts. This is space that you can use to draw your own pictures of the animals that you read about. I hope you have fun with this book and learn many new things about animals that you can see around your home and in parks near you.

THIS
IS
MY
HOME

ANTS

Ants are **insects** that are older than humans and have been on the planet for about one hundred million years before we were here.

They are found all over the world except for the areas by the North Pole and the South Pole.

Ants can carry things that weigh about three times as much as they do.

Ants are in the food chain as both **predators** and **prey.** They eat other insect eggs and they are food for birds and lizards.

Their tunnels put air in the soil and let water go right to plant roots.

They also spread seeds by storing them in their tunnels.

After ants leave an area, **fungi** and **bacteria** grow and help break down **nutrients** in the soil.

Ants can smell with their **antennae** and follow trails to find food.

Queen ants can live up to thirty years, the longest life of any insect.

BATS

Bats are the only flying **mammal**.

There are about one thousand, one hundred **species** of bats all over the world and about forty species are found in the United States.

They can live more than thirty years and can fly up to sixty miles an hour.

Many bats eat insects and they can eat over one thousand mosquitoes an hour.

They can eat their body weight in insects every night so they keep the bug population under control. This is like a person eating twenty pizzas in one night.

Some bats eat fruit or **nectar** from flowers.

A group of bats is called a colony and they are **nocturnal**.

Many bats are on the **endangered** species list because of loss of **habitat** or disease.

Some bats **migrate** and some bats **hibernate** during the winter months.

Bat droppings are called guano and are a very rich **fertilizer** for plants.

The world's smallest bat is the Bumblebee Bat which is smaller than your thumbnail and weighs less than a penny.

BEES

Honey bees have been around for millions of years.

The honeybee is the only insect that makes food for people to eat. Honey never spoils.

Bees fly to thousands of flowers to make a spoonful of honey.

A queen bee can live up to five years and all she does is fill the hive with eggs. She lays about two thousand, five hundred eggs a day.

The worker bees are all females and they are the only bees with stingers. They only sting if they feel threatened because they die once they sting.

Honeybees communicate by doing a dance for the other bees.

Bees **pollinate** most of our plants.

Honeybees never sleep and each **colony** has a different odor.

To make one pound of honey, it takes five hundred fifty-six workers and two million flowers.

Bees have two separate stomachs. One is for food and the other one is just for nectar.

One third of all the plants we eat have been pollinated by bees.

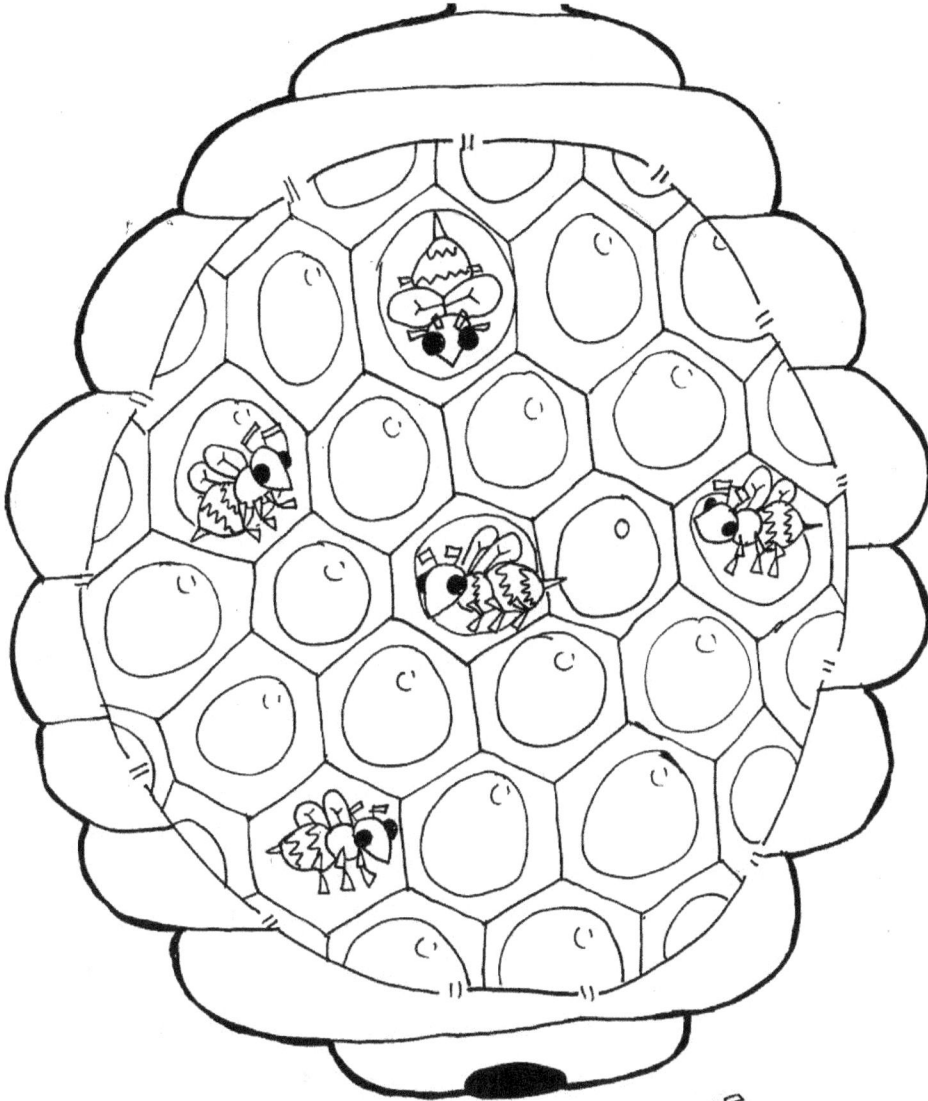

BUTTERFLIES

Butterflies taste with their feet.

And a group of butterflies is called a flutter.

Most butterflies can fly five to twelve miles an hour.

Males drink from mud puddles to get minerals that are not available in flowers. This is called "puddling."

Most butterflies feed on nectar from flowers.

The Cabbage White Butterfly is the most common butterfly in the United States.

There are more than seventeen thousand, five hundred different kinds of butterflies in the world. Seven hundred fifty kinds can be found in the United States.

Monarch butterflies **migrate** over two thousand miles to get away from the cold weather. Other butterflies migrate but don't go as far as the Monarchs.

Butterflies have tiny ears on their wings and they can tell the difference between high and low sounds.

Butterflies can't bite you because they don't have a jaw. They have a proboscis, which is like a soft drinking straw to sip on nectar and eat.

They change through a process called **metamorphosis** which goes from egg, to **caterpillar (larva)**, to **chrysalis (pupa)**, to adult butterfly.

DRAW YOUR OWN BUTTERFLY……

CARDINALS

With most kinds of birds, only the male can sing. Both male and female cardinals can sing.
 When the female cardinal sings from the nest, it usually means she is telling the male she needs more food.

The oldest Northern Cardinal ever recorded was fifteen years and nine months old. They usually live about three years.

Sometimes in the spring, male cardinals will peck on a window. It sees his reflection and thinks it is another bird coming into his **territory**.

A group of cardinals is called a "college" or a "deck."

A cardinal's favorite food is sunflower seeds and they have a strong beak so they can crack the shells. They will also eat fruits, berries, and insects.

Cardinals don't use birdhouses but will build nests in the branches of trees.

Cardinals are easy to attract to your backyard. Put feeder trays with sunflower seeds out and they will find you.

Cardinals can raise as many as three groups of eggs each summer.

CHIPMUNKS

Chipmunks are small animals that are related to squirrels.

They are about two to six inches long with a three inch tail and weigh less than a pound.

They like to eat nuts, seeds, berries, corn, mushrooms, and even plant roots and bulbs.

They live underground and dig two kinds of tunnels. One is close to the surface of the ground where they go when they are active during the day. The other kind of tunnel is deep and they go there to next, to store food, adn to spend most of the winter.

One chipmunk can gather up to one hundred sixty-five acorns in a day.

They have pouches inside their cheeks where they can store food.

A group of chipmunks is called a scurry.

The average **lifespan** of a chipmunk is between two and three years.

They have five toes on their front paws and four toes on their back paws.

Chipmunks are **diurnal** and they are **omnivores.**

CRICKET

Crickets do not make their noise by rubbing their legs together. They rub a scraping organ on one wing against a comb-like organ on the other wing.

Every cricket species has a little bit different noise-making structure that makes a special sound.

If you hear a cricket chirping, it is probably a male.

As the weather gets warmer crickets chirp more often.

Cricket's ears are tiny spots on their front legs. There are some of the smallest ears of any animal.

People in many places love crickets. Chinese people keep them for good luck. The people of Japan love their songs and in Brazil they are considered to be signs of hope.

Disney has turned them into loved creatures like Jiminy Cricket and Cri-Kee in the movie, Mulan.

Crickets often get in our homes and are usually harmless but might be annoying with their chirping.

In some countries crickets are used as a high protein food source and are eaten by humans.

Lizards, frogs, and turtles enjoy eating crickets.

A female cricket can lay up to two hundred eggs at a time.

DEER

Male deer grow new antlers every year.

A male deer is called a buck (a very large one is called a stag). A female is called a doe and a young deer is a fawn. A group of deer is called a herd.

The reason hunting jackets are neon orange is because deer can't see that color.

Their diet is made up of plants. They love berries and tender plants but they will also eat the bark of young trees.

There are over ninety different kinds of deer in the world but the most common one in the United States are the white-tailed deer and the mule-deer.

Their average lifespan is two to four years.

Deer were used by Native Americans and early settlers for both food and clothing.

White-tailed deer are the Number One game animal in the United States.

A deer has excellent hearing. This makes it hard for hunters to sneak up on it. They also have a very good sense of smell. This also helps it know if there is danger coming.

Deer can be found everywhere but Australia and Antarctica

DRAGONFLIES

Dragonflies have been around for about three hundred million years.

They love to eat mosquitoes and gnats but they don't sting and bite people.

When they first hatch they live in the water for about a year. Once they leave the water and begin to fly they only live about a month.

People in some countries like to eat them as a snack.

Having a dragonfly land on your head is considered good luck.

Groups of dragonflies are called swarms.

Predators that eat dragonflies include fish, ducks, birds, and water beetles.

They can fly about sixty miles an hour making it one of the fastest insects on the planet.

There are more than five thousand different kinds of dragonflies.

Nearly all of the dragonfly's head is eye, so they have excellent vision which helps them catch prey and also helps them avoid being caught.

One kind of dragonfly, called the "globe skinner" has the longest **migration route** of any insect. It flies eleven thousand miles back and forth across the Indian Ocean.

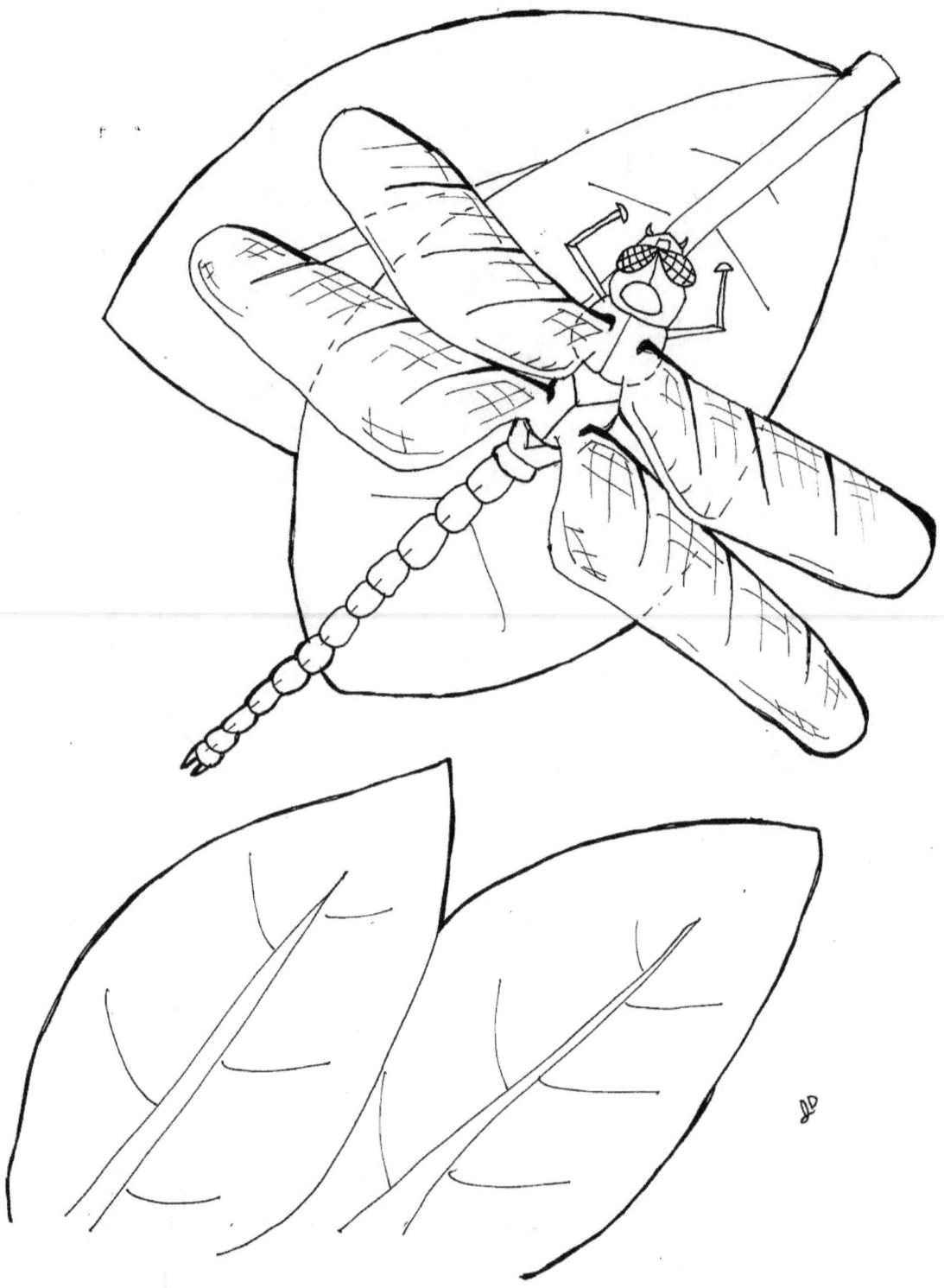

EARTHWORMS

There are about six thousand different kinds of earthworms. About one hundred eighty are found in the United States and Canada.

They can only grow so long, depending on what kind they are.

A worm has no arms, legs, or eyes.

They live where there is food, moisture, oxygen and a comfortable temperature. If they don't have these things, they go somewhere else.

In one acre of land, there can be more than a million earthworms.

Baby worms hatch from cocoons smaller than a grain of rice.

If a worm's skin dries out, it will die.

They don't have lungs or other breathing **organs** so they breathe through their skin.

Earthworms usually live one to two years.

They are found everywhere but Antarctica. Some even live in the oceans.

Each small part of the body (segment) is covered with hair-like bristles that help them wiggle through the dirt.

The castings (earthworm poop) is very good natural fertilizer for plants.

Lots of animals eat earthworms including toads, moles, birds, and snakes. In some parts of the world, people also eat them.

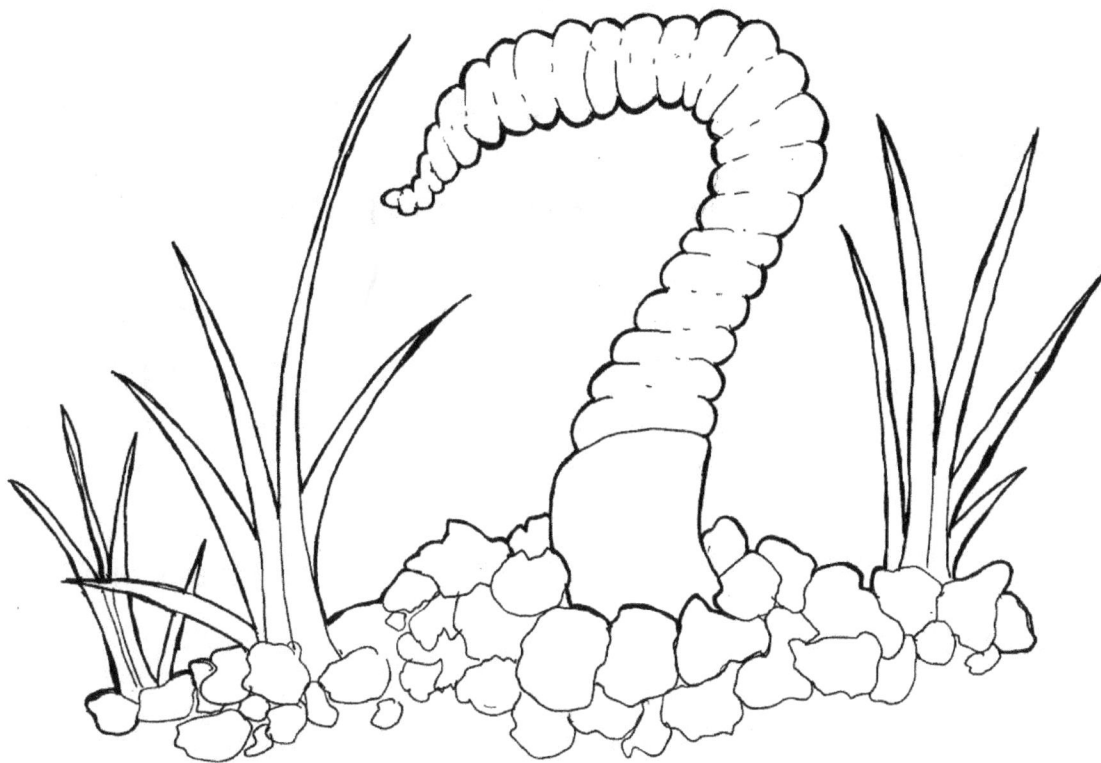

FOX

The red fox is the largest of the foxes in North America

Foxes are related to wolves and dogs but they do not run in groups or packs. They live in small families called a "leash of foxes" in underground burrows. If they don't have families to raise, they hunt and sleep alone.

They have a lot in common with cats. They are most active after the sun goes down. They hunt like a cat by stalking and pouncing. They also have sensitive whiskers, walk on their toes, have retractable claws that let them climb trees, and sometimes sleep in trees like cats.

A female fox is called a vixen, a male is called a dog, and the babies are called pups or kits.

Foxes are friendly and curious.

Foxes can live up to fourteen years.

They eat almost anything such as berries, worms, spiders, and even jam sandwiches. They often hide food to eat later.

A fox can run thirty miles per hour.

They have amazing hearing and can hear a watch ticking forty yards away.

FROGS

Frogs absorb water through their skin so they don't need to drink.

Some frogs in South America secrets a toxin (poison) that can be used on darts to kill animals when hunting. One small amount is poisonous enough to kill a human being.

A frog sheds its skin about once a week and usually eats it.

A group of frogs is called an army.

Frog's bones forms a ring when the frog is hibernating (like a tree) and scientists can use these rings to figure out the age of a frog.

The eyes and nose of a frog are on top of its head so it can breathe and see when most of its body is under the water.

Frogs usually eat bugs and worms and swallow their food whole.

Most frogs cannot live in any kind of saltwater.

Many of the brightly-colored tropical frogs are colored this way to warn predators that they are poisonous.

There are over five thousand kinds of frogs and some frog calls can be heard a mile away.

Frogs were the first land animals with vocal cords.

GRASSHOPPERS

Grasshoppers lived before dinosaurs

There are about eleven thousand kinds of grasshoppers.

Grasshoppers have two antennae, six legs, two pairs of wings and small little pinchers to tear off food such as grasses, leaves, and grain crops.

Grasshoppers are eaten as food for humans in Africa, Central America, and South America. They are a very good source of protein.

Grasshoppers have ears on their bellies or abdomens.

Grasshoppers can fly.

They jump by using their back knees as a spring to push them into the air.

A grasshopper eats about half of its body weight in plants every day. When they gather in large groups they can cause billions of dollars worth of damage to food crops every year.

GROUNDHOGS

Groundhogs are also known as woodchucks.

They are related to squirrels, chipmunks, and prairie dogs.

They dig long tunnels about five feet underground and usually have five openings in their burrows so they can escape from predators. Their claws make them a good digger. They even have a separate "bathroom chamber" in their burrows.

They usually weigh about twelve to fifteen pounds. Their diets are greens, fruits, and vegetables. They are good swimmers and tree climbers.

They are a very clean animals that live for about five or six years.

Groundhogs are found only in North America. They are solitary animals who can eat about a pound of food at a time.

They hibernate in the winter.

They have one **litter** of babies a year with two to nine pups born in March or April.

Baby groundhogs are born naked, blind, and helpless and are only about four inches long.

They stay with their mother for about six weeks.

HAWKS

Hawks are **birds of prey** that have sharp talons (claws), a large curved bill, and muscular legs. They have excellent eyesight and can see eight times better than humans.

A red-tailed hawk can fly between twenty and forty miles per hour but a peregrine falcon can fly up to sixty miles per hour.

The smallest hawk is the Sparrow Hawk and weighs about three ounces. The largest hawk, weighs up to five pounds.

Hawks are able to see different colors.

Hawks can dive one hundred fifty miles per hour and can catch prey both in the air and on the ground.

They are active during the day and they hunt and eat whatever is available (Frogs, squirrels, rats, snakes, and rabbits)

Average lifespan of a hawk is between thirteen and twenty years in the wild.

There are more than two hundred species of hawks and they are found everywhere but Antarctica.

When hawks gather in a group it is called a "kettle of hawks." A kettle might contain thousands of birds. They usually live alone but hawks that migrate take advantage of large groups to find warm **wind currents.**

MICE

A mouse is a small rodent that has a pointed snout (nose) , small rounded ears, and a long tail.

There are more than thirty different kinds of mice.

Mice are usually active at night. They have poor eyesight buy very good senses of hearing and smell.

In the wild, mice are **herbivores** that eat all kinds of fruit and grains from plants.

A mouse will eat fifteen to twenty times a day and build their homes close to a food source.

Mice usually only live about six months in the wild because they have so many animals that hunt them.

There are some places in the world where mice are eaten as a source of protein by humans.

Mice are very friendly and clean. They create separate places to put their food, to sleep, and to use as a bathroom when put in a cage and raised as a pet.

A group of mice is called a "mischief."

Males are called bucks, females are called does and the baby mice are called kittens or sometimes they are called Pinkys.

OPOSSUM

It is the only **marsupial** found north of Mexico.

It is generally referred to as a "possum."

There are sixty different kinds of possums and none of them are endangered.

They are about fifteen to twenty inches long and weight between four and twelve pounds.

They are one of the oldest types of mammals and were here on Earth when the dinosaurs were.

Possums have more teeth than any other mammal with fifty teeth.

They are omnivores. Insects are on their diet as well as frogs, eggs, fruit, and berries. They also eat **carrion.**

They don't' get sick very often and will not get rabies. They move constantly to look for food and they use abandoned dens and shelters for their home.

They hunt at night and have poor eyesight but an excellent sense of smell.

A group of possums is called a "passel."

Baby possums are about the size of a honeybee when they are born. One litter has about twenty babies and only a few survive. They crawl to their mother's pouch and stay there for about two months.

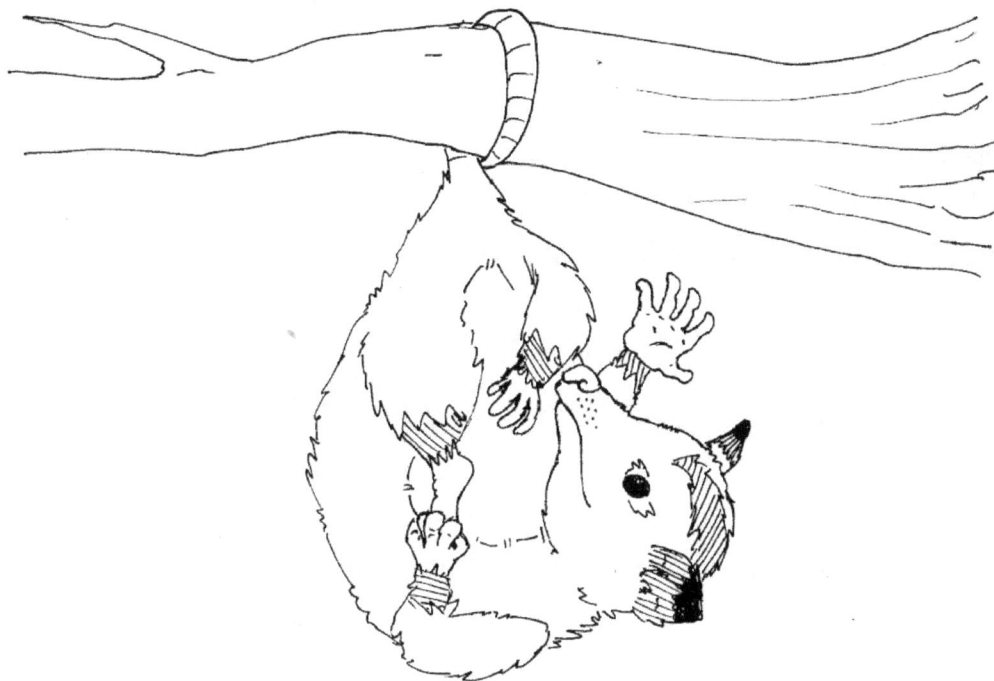

OWLS

There are about two hundred different kinds of owls.

They are active at night and hunt insects, small animals, like mice, and other birds.

A group of owls is called a parliament.

Owls have very powerful **talons** which help them catch and kill their prey

The tiniest owl is the Elf Owl which is five to six inches and weighs about one and a half ounces. The largest owl, the Great Gray Owl, is thirty-two inches tall.

Some owls can see their prey up to a half a mile away.

Owls make no noise when they fly.

They swallow their prey whole then throw up the bones and fur in a small pellet.

Owls feed the strongest babies first if there is not much food available.

The colors and markings on their feathers help them blend in well with their surroundings.

In Japan there are owl cafes where you can hang out with owls while drinking tea.

RACCOONS

Raccoons can make over fifty different sounds.

Raccoons have three or four babies in a litter.

Raccoons hands look like a human's. They have five fingers one which is like our thumb.

They eat both plant material and animals. They often place their food in water before they eat it, appearing to wash it.

They live in a hollow tree or any place they can find for shelter.

Raccoons live on their own and hunt at night.

They don't hibernate but spend cold winter days in their **burrows.**

A group of raccoons is called a "nursery" or a "gaze"

The live about five years in the wild.

Raccoons have a black mask around their eyes and rings on their tail. They weight around twenty pounds.

Baby raccoons are known as cubs or kits. They stay near their mothers for the first year of life and then they become entirely independent.

SKUNK

Skunks are small mammals that are usually recognized by their black and white colored fur. They can be from ten to twenty inches in size and weigh up to fourteen pounds.

There are ten kinds of skunks and almost all live in North and Central America.

They are omnivores, eating both plants and animals. They like fruits, insects, grubs, and grass. They will often attack a beehive because they eat honey bees.

They have a scent gland that can release a foul smelling chemical when trying to get a predator to go away. Before it sprays the victim, skunks will turn its back, lift its tail, start hissing, and stomping with its feet. All warning signs to get the predator to back off. Once they spray, it can go up to ten feet.

Their worst enemies are coyotes, bobcats, and owls.

The males are called bucks, the females are called does, and the babies are called kits.

Skunks have poor eyesight but excellent smell and hearing.

They can live up to three years in the wild.

They rarely travel more than two miles from their dens and will be found close to a water supply. They make their homes in hollow trees and brush piles.

SNAKES

Snakes can't bite food so they have to swallow it whole. They have flexible jaws which allow them to eat prey bigger than their head.

They are found everywhere but Antarctica.

Some species use **venom** to hunt and kill their prey.

There are about seven hundred twenty-five kinds of snakes and about two hundred fifty can kill a human with one bite.

It typically takes a snake three to five days to digest its meal.

Some animals, like the mongoose, are not affected by a snake bite.

To avoid predators, some snakes poop whenever they want. They make themselves so dirty and smelly that predators run away.

Humans have twenty-four ribs. Some snakes can have more than four hundred.

There are about three thousand different kinds of snakes and all of them are predators. They are **carnivores**.

Scales cover every inch of a snake's body, even its eyes.

The most common snake in North America is the garter snake.

A snake's **fangs** usually last about six to ten weeks. When a fang wears out, a new one grows in its place.

SPIDERS

Spiders are arachnids, not insects. They have eight legs while insects have six. They don't have antennae and insects do. They have two body parts and insects have three.

Spiders are found everywhere but Antarctica.

There are about thirty-eight thousand species of spiders.

Spiders eat more insects than birds and bats combined.

All spiders spin silk, but not all spiders spin webs.

Abandoned spider webs are called "cobwebs."

Spiders have blue blood and most only live for about a year.

Arachnophobia is the fear of spiders and is the most common fear.

The silk in a spider's web is five times stronger than a strand of steel that is the same thickness.

Spiders do not have teeth so they cannot chew their food. Instead, they inject digestive juices into the inside of their meal and suck up the mushy insides.

Some male spiders give dead flies to the females as presents.

The bird-dropping spider gets its name because it looks like bird poop. This type of camouflage prevents birds from eating it.

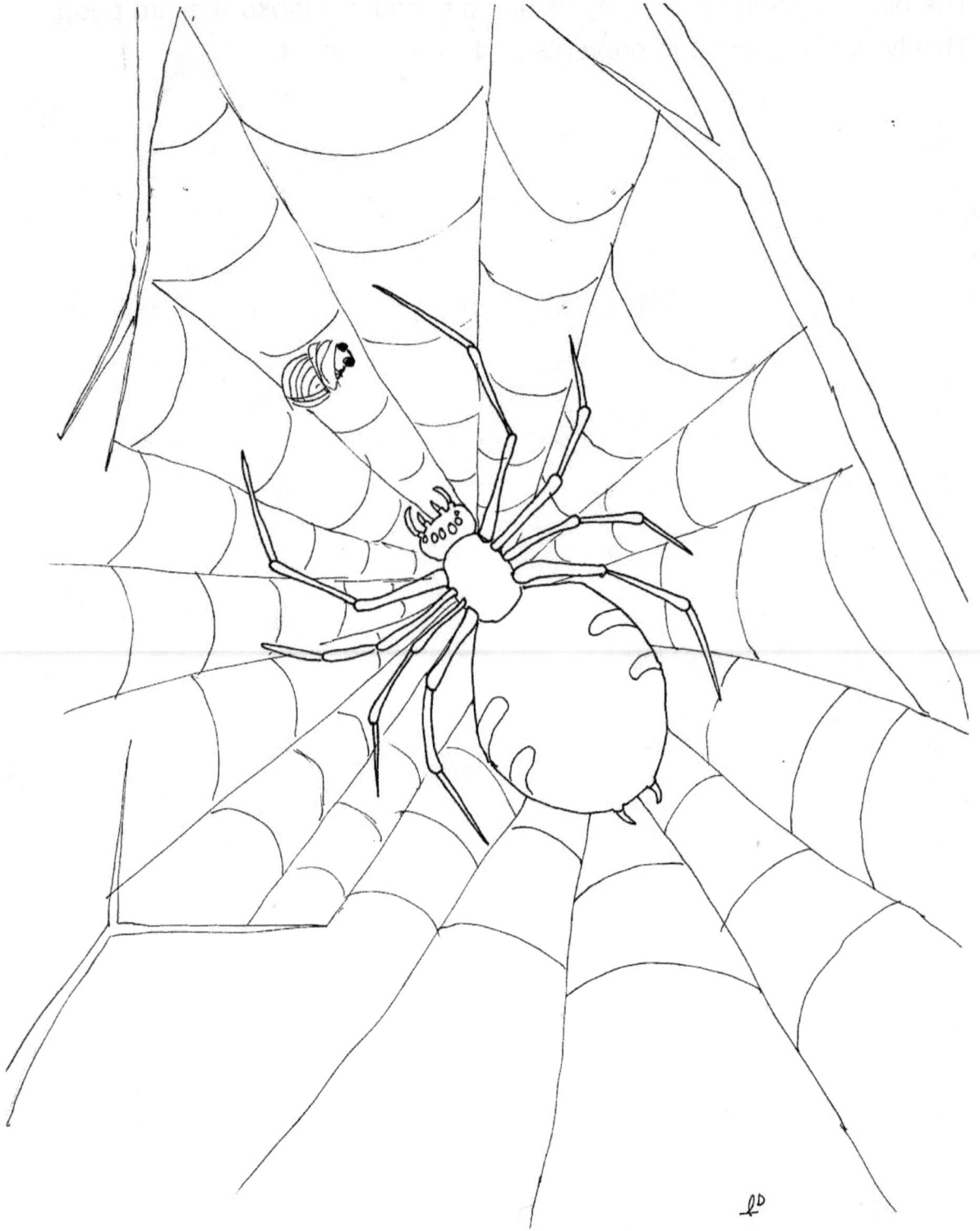

SQUIRRELS

There are two hundred eighty-five species of squirrels and they are found everywhere but Australia and Antarctica.

Squirrels have one litter of babies a year with two to four babies per litter.

They can eat their own body weight every week.

They can fall about one hundred feet without hurting themselves. When jumping, or falling, they use their tail both for balance and as a parachute.

Squirrels can jump up to twenty feet. They have long hind legs and short front legs that help them leap that distance.

Some squirrels can smell food under a foot of snow.

A squirrel's front teeth never stop growing and they have to gnaw to keep their teeth at the right length.

Squirrels run in a zigzag pattern trying to escape predators.

Squirrels don't' dig up all of their buried nuts and some begin to grow and become new trees.

Baby squirrels will only pee and poop in their mother's mouth so that she can dispose of the waste outside the nest and keep predators from smelling the scent.

When a squirrel thinks it is being watched it pretends to bury something.

TOADS

Toads lay their eggs in water but they do not need to live near water to survive.

They have rough dry bumpy skin and do not have many predators.

A group of toads is called a "knot."

Like frogs, toads start out life as **tadpoles**.

Toads do not have teeth, so they don't chew food, they swallow it whole.

They are active at night and feed on insects and usually burrow under the ground during the day.

They hibernate during the winter and live about three to five years in the wild.

The color of a toad's skin changes depending on the soil of its habitat.

They are carnivores and have a diet of insects, spiders, and earthworms.

The adult male croaks but the female toads do not make any sound.

Adult females can lay two thousand to twenty thousand eggs.

One toad can eat up to one thousand insects every day.

The main predators of toads are snakes.

TURTLES

Turtles belong to one of the oldest reptile groups in the world. They date back to the time of dinosaurs over two hundred million years ago.

A turtle's body is made up of over fifty bones. The shell grows with them.

What a turtle eats depends on its environment. Land turtles munch on beetles, fruit, and grass.

Baby turtles begin life as meat eaters but eat more plants as they grow older.

They live a very long time, sometimes ever one hundred years, depending on the species.

Of the three hundred species of turtles and tortoises, one hundred twenty-nine are endangered.

They don't have a very good sense of hearing but they can hear when predators are near.

They can see colors and things which are red, orange, or yellow seem to attract them the most.

They are not social and do not spend time with other turtles. They are active during the day.

All turtles lay eggs. Baby turtles are called "Sparkies. Turtles never come out of their shell and a group of turtles is often called a "bale."

WOODPECKERS

There are more than one hundred eighty species of woodpeckers and they have a lot of different habitats.

There are only about two dozen woodpecker species found in the United States. The downy woodpecker is the most common backyard woodpecker.

They will nest in birdhouses and roost boxes.

The most common colors for all woodpeckers are black, white, red, and yellow.

Woodpeckers eat bugs, sap, nuts, fruit, and seeds.

Woodpeckers can peck up to twenty times per second or about ten thousand times a day, usually looking for food.

The average lifespan is four to twelve years. Larger woodpeckers live longer, sometimes up to twenty or thirty years.

The greatest threat to woodpeckers is loss of habitat to development and insecticide that eliminates food sources.

Woodpeckers have very long tongues to reach insects inside trees.

Both males and females are able to drum trees and use it to communicate.

Native Americans used the bills of woodpeckers as decorations and to trade.

GLOSSARY

ANTS

- Antenna - one of two or four small feelers on the head of insects (antennae is the plural form of the word)
- Bacteria - one-celled organism that can only be seen with a microscope
- Fungi - living organism that is not a plant, an animal, or a bacteria (example is a mushroom or mold)
- Insect - a very small animal with three body parts and three pairs of legs. Some have one or two pairs of wings too.
- Nutrients - something that provides nourishment or food necessary to grow
- Predator - an animal that hunts a smaller weaker animal
- Prey - an animal being hunted, caught, and eaten by another animal

BATS

- Endangered - Any type of plant or animal that is in danger of disappearing forever.
- Fertilizer - a substance used to make soil grow plants better
- Habitat - the home of a plant or animal
- Hibernate - when animals find a safe place to stay until winter ends. They barely breathe and their body temperature goes down.
- Mammal - an animal with a backbone that feeds its young milk made by the mother and have skin covered at some time in their life with hair or fur
- Migrate - movement of animals from one region to another for feeding or breeding
- Nectar - sweet liquid produced by plants and used for food and making honey

- Nocturnal - active during nighttime
- Species - a group of animals closely related to each other aht can breed and produce babies

BEES

- Colony - a group of the same kind of plants or animals that live and grow together
- Pollinate - to take pollen between plants so they can make seeds and food

BUTTERFLIES

- Caterpillar - worm-like larva of an insect
- Chrysalis - the pupa stage before becoming a butterfly
- Larva - the young stage of some animals
- Metamorphosis - process that some animals go through in stages ro become an adult
- Pupa - Stage of development after the larva stage before becoming an adult

CARDINALS

- Territory - a region that is marked and defended by a certain kind of animal for food and breeding

CHIPMUNKS

- Diurnal - Active during the day
- Lifespan - the average length of life for a plant or animal
- Omnivores - an animal that eats both plants and animals for their main food source

DRAGONFLY

- Migration route - the route usually used by animals to move from one region to another

EARTHWORMS
- Organs - parts of plants or animals that perform a particular job

GROUNDHOGS
- Litter - the number of babies in one birth cycle

HAWKS
- Birds of Prey - Birds that hunt other animals such as mice for food
- Wind currents - gigantic air currents

MICE
- Herbivores - an animal that gets its food from plants and only plants
- Rodent - mammals with long sharp front teeth used for gnawing

OPOSSUM
- Carrion - dead and rotting flesh of an animal
- Marsupial - group of mammals that carry their young in a pouch

OWLS
- Talons - claws

RACCOONS
- Burrows - tunnels underground

SNAKE
- Carnivores - animals that eat only meat and meat products such as eggs
- Fangs - a long sharp tooth that is used to do harm
- Venom - a substance that is poisonous

TOADS
- Tadpoles - the larva of a toad or frog that has a long tail, breathes with gills, and lives in water